The Demons of Deception

Rituals to Hide the Truth, Create Confusion and Conceal Your Actions

Corwin Hargrove

All Rights Reserved. This book may not be copied, reproduced, in whole or in part, in any form or by any means electronic or mechanical, or by any method now known or hereafter invented, without written permission from Corwin Hargrove.

All images in this book are subject to copyright. Where traditional sources have been used, they have been crafted into entirely new images, and may not be copied or shared, commercially or gratis.

Disclaimer: The content of this book is based on personal experience and conjecture and should be regarded as speculative entertainment and not professional, medical or personal advice. The concepts and practices presented here are to be used at your own risk. Corwin Hargrove is not responsible for the experiences you obtain from working with the methods presented. It is hereby stated clearly and in full that the author neither suggests nor condones that you ever act in a way that can cause harm, and this book is provided with the understanding that the materials be used in accordance with the laws of your country or any country in which you are present.

Copyright © 2017 Corwin Hargrove

If you obtained a pirated copy of this book, you would be wise to discard it and pay for the real thing.

TABLE of CONTENTS

The Deceptive Truth	7
The Nature of Demons and Sigils	13
The Structure of the Sigils	17
The Preparation	19
The Ritual	25
The Veil of Secrecy	33
To Hide the Past	35
To Reduce Personal Suspicion	39
To Reduce Perception of Your Actions	43
To Bring Silence	47
The Shadow of False Beliefs	51
To Appear Plausible	53
To Appear Trustworthy	57
To Encourage False Beliefs	61
To Seem Believable Under Scrutiny	65
The Flame of Confusion	69
To Confuse an Individual	71
To Bring General Confusion	75
To Discourage Clarity of Thought	79
To Encourage Forgetfulness	83
The Mask of Concealment	87
To Become Less Visible	89
To Distract Attention	93
To Blur the Truth	97
To Move Attention to Another	101
Ongoing Magick	105

The Deceptive Truth

Secrecy is power. Whatever actions you take in the world, you cannot afford to be picked apart by those who would take what is precious to you. With deception on your side, you can dominate your fortune.

Deception is a way to hide your actions and to control how much truth people see. Whether you're having an affair or trying to keep important business secrets, I doubt you need me to tell you how powerful secrecy can be. The wise know that secrecy is the ultimate protection against the efforts of an enemy. This magick gives you the power to work in the world as you wish to work.

The sigils in this book contain over one hundred and sixty individual demonic seals, crafted into thirty-two magickal sigils, giving you access to Sixteen Powers of Secrecy.

The demons revealed in this book are well known to occultists, but they are not the demons found most commonly in books of demonic practice. What you get in this book is quite unique, and the ritual process brings a cunning simplicity that makes the old grimoires seem almost primitive.

With *The Veil of Secrecy* you can hide the past, reduce suspicion, reduce perception of your actions, and bring silence to those who know your secrets.

Using *The Shadow of False Beliefs* you can appear plausible or trustworthy while encouraging falsities to arise in the minds of other people, and make those who question you believe every answer you give.

The Flame of Confusion enables you to confuse an individual, bring general confusion, discourage clarity of thought and encourage forgetfulness.

The Mask of Concealment lets you become less visible, to distract attention, to blur the truth or even to move attention away from yourself to another person.

Information is power, and when information is cloaked in secrecy, your enemies are foiled. This aspect of the power should not be underestimated. Enemies love knowledge. In an age when everything is shared, we are made weak by constant revelations. If this means nothing to you, and you have no enemies, know that there will come a time when somebody has power over you, because of what they know. It may be your boss, an employee, a jealous lover or anybody who wants to bring you harm and disruption. Being able to hide the truth from an enemy is extremely useful. One throwaway example; going through a difficult divorce is much easier when the other party has no ability to hold on to evidence that could be used against you. Confuse that person, and you come out on top.

Secrecy and deception are useful even when there are no enemies, and when protection is not of such importance. I have helped people use magick to hide their personal history from new lovers, so that they can move on without having to explain past mistakes, addictions and even crimes. I have helped people deceive with charm, to gain advantage in interviews, in competitions and in business.

Deception can even be used to lead others to fail, so that you succeed. When you are trusted, people invest in you and your business. Even when you are new to an industry or field of work, you can be seen as an expert. You can appeal to the better nature of people, or make them have doubts that undermine the people that you wish to fail. When you have taken actions that you regret, the relief of deception and the ability to cover your tracks is obvious, but the powers in this book give you many more advantages that are not so obvious.

Deception can give you the ability to live life the way you want to live it, without being doubted, questioned or troubled, and it can protect you, and give you the ability to dominate others and suppress their power. I will allow you to use your own imagination to find applications for this magick. As you read through the book and see the individual rituals, the true depth of this magick should be revealed to you.

If you wring your hands over the morals of deception, then you're in good company, because only an idiot would use magick to deceive without first giving it some thought. A touch of hand-wringing is wise. But if you work yourself up into a frenzy of fear about working with demons, this book is not for you. Demons are obliged to work for you, and when called in this manner they do not have the power to throw the furniture around and ruin your life or make you pay them back. But I know that for every person who gets results with demons, there will be another who worries that every tiny accident is a demonic backlash. This is your business, not mine. If you have any reservations about demonic work, please stop reading now.

If you *are* willing to work with demons, know that this method has been constructed to keep the demons fully under your control, working only in the way that you wish. This is achieved by using a mix of demonic calls and sigils of power. The demons are powerful, but they are not the out-of-control beasts that many would have you believe. And in this system, you are not calling them to visible appearance. You only instruct them to help with deception, and that is all that they will do.

The magick is based around calling the names of various combinations of demons, while gazing upon their seals, which are built into sigils. The sigils have been constructed around an offset seven-pointed star, designed to bring discord to the perception of others. Although the sigils are unique to this book, you can find versions of the demonic seals themselves in books such as Joseph Peterson's version of *The Lesser Key of Solomon*, or even the one by S. L. MacGregor Mathers, and you may be inclined to see other versions of the seals in *The Goetia of Dr. Rudd* by Stephen Skinner and David Rankine. Truth be told, it's easy to get all the seals in this book with some messing about online. But what do you do with these scribbled seals? That's the mystery. If you follow the instructions in the old grimoires, you'll be working with a watery, withered magick that lacks real direction and instruction. And you'll be working for a long time, without results. By using the combined sigils that are unique to this book, and the method presented here, you can get demonic magick working with minimal drama.

Somebody said my first book, *The Magick of Influence*, was an attempt to dumb down the old grimoires so that they are suitable for idiots. I respectfully disagree, because I do not class my readers as idiots, and because the old grimoires are so obscure and unworkable that discerning how to get actual results from those weird ramblings can take years. The grimoires are often a smokescreen to their own wisdom. But creative occultists have found that there is power in the grimoires, and that these demons can be called easily, and that their powers are many. This particular class of demons can be called to work on anything you wish, according to the old texts, but it is true that one power works more readily than any other. That power is deception.

It would be a falsehood to claim that the demons in this book are *only* able to work on deception. It is claimed in the source grimoire itself that they can be brought to bear on *any* problem, and there is truth in this. But they work on deception *most easily*. It could even be claimed that deception is integral to their other subtler workings, and as such, in this book I treat them purely as demons of deception.

If you are only vaguely familiar with the occult, and have heard of *goetia*, or *goetic demons*, or anything similar, then you've probably heard about the demons of *Goetia*, the first and most infamous book of *The Lesser Key of Solomon* (also known as *Lemegeton, Clavicula Salomonis Regis* and many other modern titles). We are not concerned with that book here, or the seventy-two famous demons it contains. The demons in *this* book are from the second book of *The Lesser Key of Solomon*, known as *Theurgia-Goetia*. The demons are described as 'aerial spirits' with natures that are both 'good and evil.' Some occultists would insist that these spirits are, as stated, mere aerial spirits and not demons at all. I believe that it is certainly fair to say these spirits are not angels, and a book called *Aerial Spirits of Deception* would be misleading to readers. Spirits that embody evil as part of their nature are, to most people, demons. In fairness to those who disagree with me, the distinction between angels and demons is something people obsess about today, but in the past, there were many spirits that were not so readily or obsessively labeled – so it doesn't really matter what you call them, if you are willing to work with them. Today, most encyclopedias and other sources list and name these aerials spirits as demons, and I believe they are right to do so. The spirits *act* as demons; fast, directly and as you command them to act.

Although *Theurgia-Goetia* is readily available, it is not remotely as popular as the *Goetia*. The aerial demons are rarely used, and there isn't the same excitement about them in the occult community. This is probably because the grimoire instructions were so vague, that it requires a great deal of decoding and experimentation to discover how to use them. In this book, you get a ritual process that works for these demons. The coded instructions, which were banal and ineffective, have been decoded, reconstructed and made into something that works.

The ritual process is relatively simple, with combinations of sigils and demon calls giving you direct access to your desired result.

It has been known in occult circles for some time that combining names of spirits in patterns can yield results. In 2015, Damon Brand revealed one of the preserved secrets of magick, quietly releasing a book called *Words of Power* which exposed the practical application of this method, if not the theory. Although popular, very few people know the depth of this revelation. His book showed that *combinations* of angelic names can be a form of ritualistic encoding, so that you do nothing but say a list of angelic names in a certain order, and that unlocks your result. What he failed to mention is that the same style of encoding works for demons.

That principle is used here, though I must admit that it is not quite so simple. In this book, there is more ceremony, and an additional layer of mental preparation, along with a small amount of paraphernalia. The core technique is quite similar, because you scan your eyes over an arrangement of demonic seals, and then say the names of the demons. The specific arrangement of the ruling demons, in relation to their subordinates, encodes the nature of your result.

The book doesn't cover every aspect of secrecy and deception, but I've taken the primary powers of this class of demons, and shown how they can be applied to sixteen forms of occult dishonesty and concealment. You get that, and nothing else. I'm not prepared to dress up the book with invented spells and rituals to make it more complete. What's here is good enough for most purposes.

Take care to know that dark magick is not about *being* evil, and as stated at the outset, deception is a tool that is used by the cunning and clever, not those who wish to bask in the pseudo-drama of the evil occultist. Truly evil people find ways to manipulate and cause harm *without* magick, *with* magick, or with any other device that is to hand. I can imagine this magick being used for very dark purposes, but I trust that the canny do not dwell in deception; they live fully and openly where possible, using deception with purpose and for protection, not as a lifestyle. But use the magick as you will, and live with your own consequences.

The Nature of Demons and Sigils

You may be tempted to rush into the practical process, but to avoid confusion I suggest that you pay attention to the following descriptions of the demons and the sigils.

There are four Emperor Demons known as Carnesiel, Caspiel, Amenadiel and Demoriel. In this book, each Emperor Demon rules over four individual rituals. In each of those rituals you speak your command to a Demon of Adjuration.

The Emperor Demon Carnesiel rules over the Demons of Adjuration known as Pamersiel, Padiel, Camuel and Aschiel.

The Emperor Demon Caspiel rules over the Demons of Adjuration known as Barmiel, Gediel, Asyriel and Maseriel.

The Emperor Demon Amenadiel rules over the Demons of Adjuration known as Malgaras, Dorochiel, Usiel and Cabariel.

The Emperor Demon Demoriel rules over the Demons of Adjuration known as Rasiel, Symiel, Armadiel and Baruchas.

For each ritual, there are two sigils – one for the Emperor Demon (and related subordinate demons) and one for the Demon of Adjuration (and related subordinate demons).

In the first sigil, the large central circle (which obscures most of the star) contains the seal of the Emperor Demon that rules over all the other demons in the ritual. Surrounding this demonic seal are the seals of lesser demons, drawn so that their base is angled toward the center of the circle.

If you look at the first ritual, for example, it calls on Pamersiel under Carnesiel. This means that in the first sigil, it is the Demon Emperor Carnesiel's sigil that dominates the large central circle. Surrounding Carnesiel are the seals of Orich, Zabriel, Buchafas, Arisiel, Bedary, Laphor and Vadriel. These demons work for Carnesiel and help open the gateway to Pamersiel.

THE INNER CIRCLE CONTAINS THE SEAL OF THE DEMON EMPEROR. IN THIS EXAMPLE IT IS CARNESIEL

When using the actual rituals, the demon names are not visible in the sigil, and they are provided here only to illustrate how the sigil is constructed.

There are sixteen rituals in this book, and in each ritual, there is a Demon of Adjuration. This demon may be a King, Prince or Duke, but whatever the title, this demon always works below The Emperor Demon, with its own subordinates. This makes it the ideal demon for you to approach – it will work your magick with the authority and power of the demons above it, and the large workforce of demons below it.

For each ritual, the second sigil contains a relatively small central circle, so that the offset seven-pointed star is more readily visible. In the central circle, you find the seal of the Demon of Adjuration. This demon is, of course, ruled by the Emperor Demon from the previous sigil, but has power over the lesser demons in the second sigil. The seals are arranged around the central circle, but all are upright rather than angled. Symbolically, this shows that *your* power is an important part of the ritual (the demons are arranged for ease of viewing by *you*), and that these demons are not just listening to commands from above, but are opening to you, your needs and your desires.

In this example of the second sigil, the seal of the **Demon of Adjuration**, Pamersiel, is in the center of the circle. Around the outside you find the seals of the subordinate demons, Anoyr, Madriel, Ebras, Ormenus, Rablion, Abrulges and Madres. This is illustrated here:

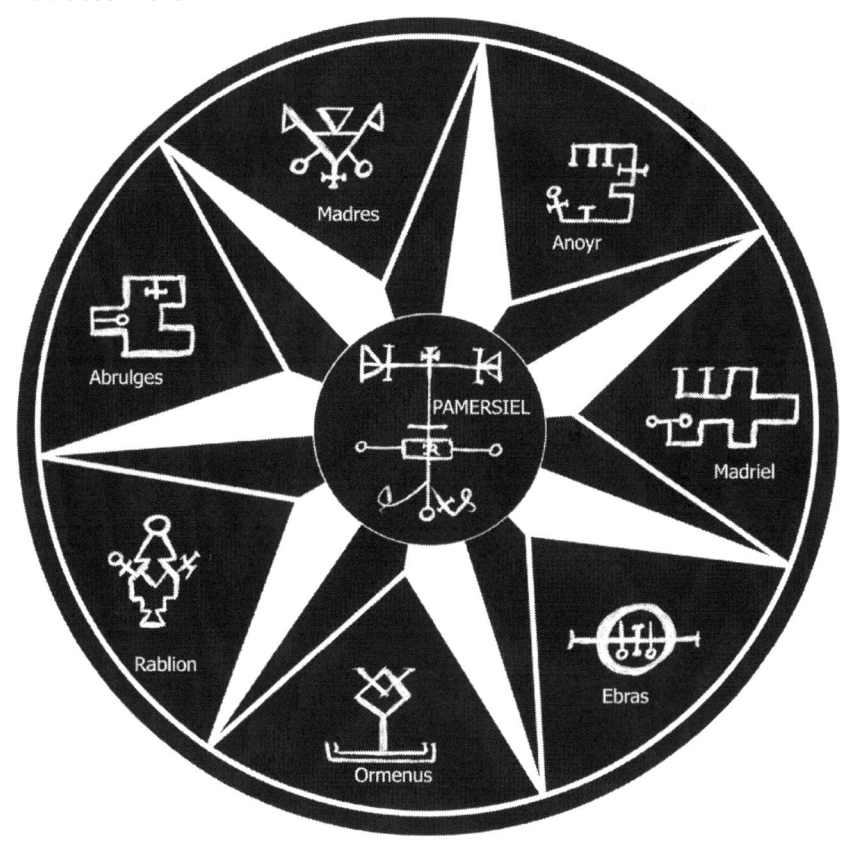

Again, when using the ritual sigil, the demon names are not visible, as this is merely an illustration.

As you can see, you are calling on a hierarchy of demons,

so that there is a flow of power, with each level working to help you. Rather than working from the lower levels first, to eventually reach the spirits at the top (as you might with, say, angelic magick), you speak straight to those at the top and get them to shake their subordinates into action. This works, because the great Emperor Demons are easily called, roused and made conscious of you and your desire.

You should also take note that the word 'adjuration' can sometimes be taken to mean something like 'to beg,' but it does not mean that here. When used in relation to a Demon of Adjuration, it means only that you make an earnest request. The demon is called a Demon of Adjuration purely because this is the demon to whom you make your earnest request. You are not begging or pleading or adoring. You're telling the demon what you truly want, and you expect the demon to assist, because it is the demon's office to do so.

Perhaps none of this background material matters, of itself, but I have taken the time to share it because if you don't know it, you might wonder, and ponder, and find that you get wrapped up in thinking all about this material. It isn't important, per se, but a little knowledge about the theory can make it easier to let go of speculation, and get on with the magick itself.

The Structure of the Sigils

To aid your practice, you may wish to know that in each sigil, the subordinate demons are placed in a clockwise fashion, starting at the top right. This becomes important when you scan the sigils visually. The scanning technique itself is explained later, but it may help to know that in the first sigil, you first scan the seal in the central circle, then you move to the top right, and scan the seals clockwise around the circle. In this example, you would start with Carnesiel in the center, then move to the top right for Orich, and continue clockwise until you reach Vadriel.

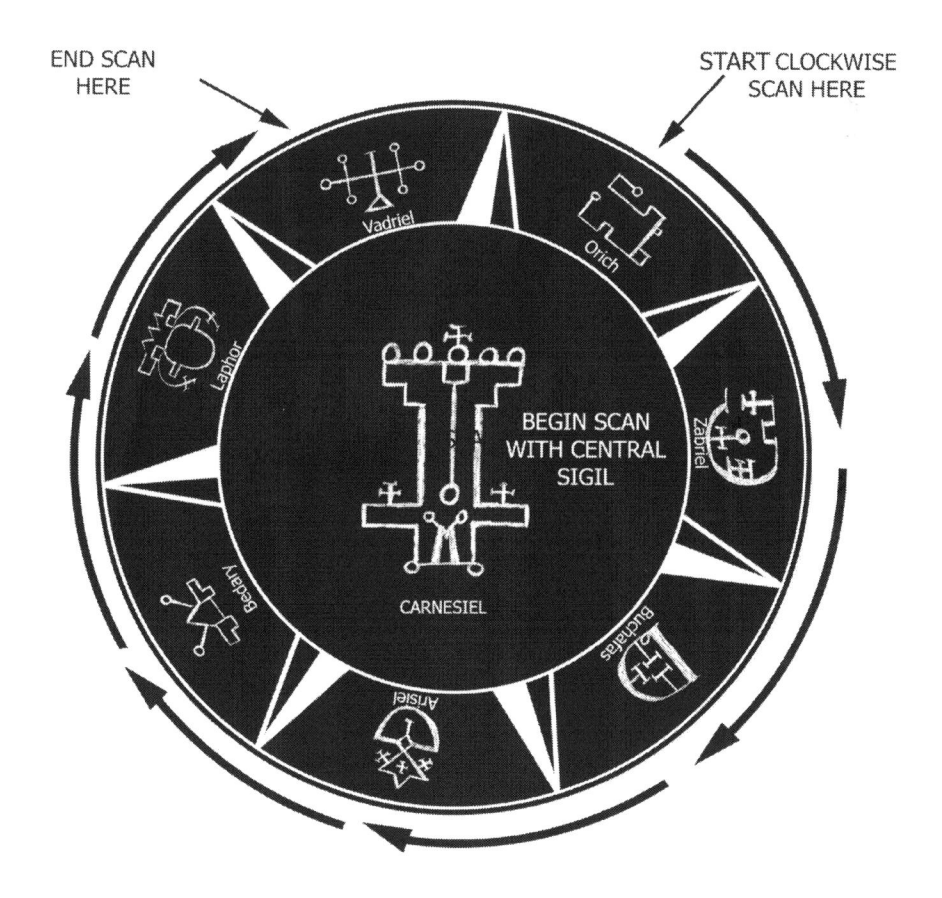

In the second sigil, the central circle contains the seal of the Demon of Adjuration for your chosen ritual. In this example, it is

Pamersiel. You would scan Pamersiel in the center first, then move to Anoyr on the top right, and continue clockwise until you reach Madres.

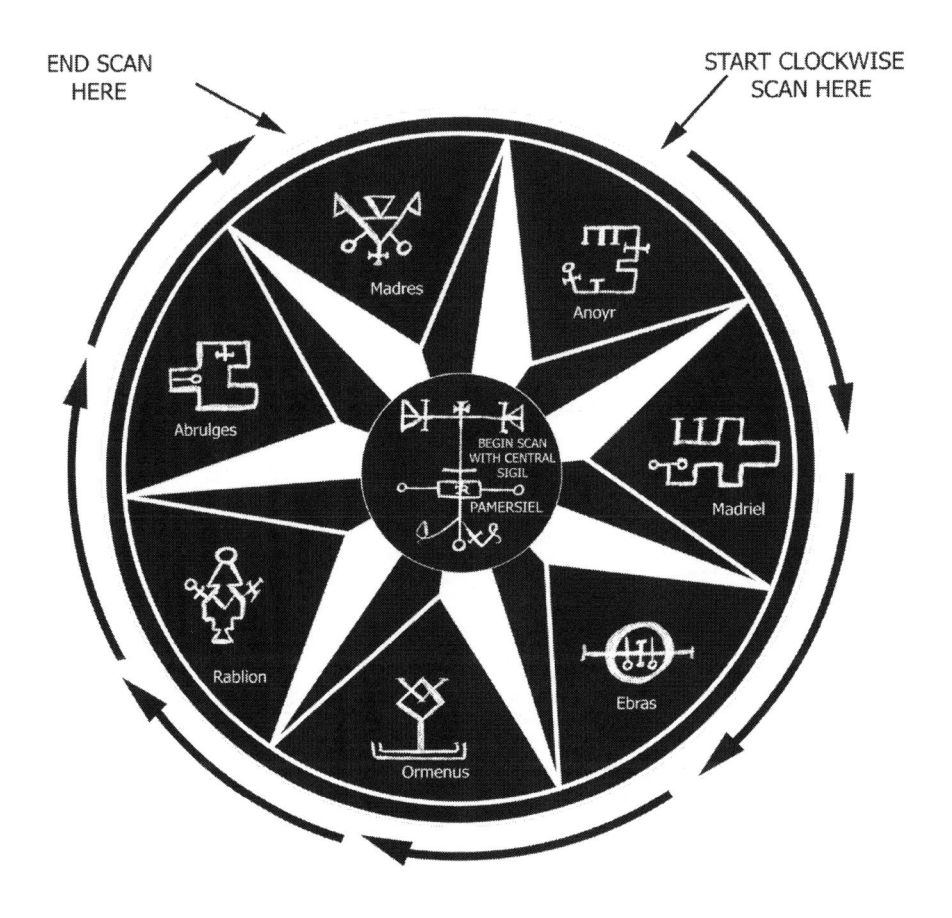

This basic structure is useful to know, but the scanning technique will be explored in depth in a later chapter. For now, you have more than enough theory and background information.

The Preparation

In theory, you can perform magick anywhere at any time, and it will work. Some styles of magick respond best when you face a particular direction, or work during a certain hour, or during a particular astrological phase. The magick in this book is concerned more with the state of mind you enter. Even the old grimoires agree with me on this, more or less. Some will find that statement laughable, as a glance through the old grimoire can make it seem that the emphasis of this magick is entirely on facing certain directions at particular times. Let me suggest that you try this book's method, and ignore the smokescreen of details from the old grimoire. Let go of dogma. The magick works when you want it to work.

I suggest working in the evening, or late at night, but this is only because it provides a better atmosphere for dark magick. Some of the demons are supposedly linked to the night, but experience shows that they *can* be called during the day, even if the grimoire insists otherwise – I guess it's always night somewhere in the world. But your own night is the best time to work this demonic magick. If the only time you get to work the magick is noon, then close out the light as much as possible, and do what you can to let the atmosphere become darker.

You are not trying to make it frightening, but the atmosphere should be heavier, and darkness helps with that. There's never a completely ideal situation. I once went to an island off the coast of Scotland, expecting it to have dark and mystical overtones ideal for magick, but it felt so pleasant and peaceful that dark magick felt wrong, and it was easier to wait until I got home. I've had great success working in noisy cities.

Work at night. About an hour before you begin, dampen the noise; turn off phones, computers, the TV. The magick should not be slotted into your routine, but should be the focus of the time set out before you. Give the magick some space and it works better, because you are able to get into it more deeply. (This is why so many rituals contain bathing and cleansing and all that preparation – the spirits don't care a damn about all that, but it gives you time to lower yourself into the ritual and the mindset of the ritual.) There's no need to bathe, but find an hour or so of quiet, calm time before the ritual begins, alone with your quiet thoughts. If you can't find an hour to settle into a ritual, you're probably not cut out for magick.

Or, you live in a house with six other people and never get time to yourself. Ok, you work it as well as you can. You tell everybody that you don't want to be disturbed for a couple of hours. Privacy is not easy. The best way to do this magick is alone, speaking the words loudly and with force, in a quiet place, where your words are the only sound. If you can't do that, you have a couple of options. One is to whisper, but that feels so pathetic and defensive; it's the opposite of bold. A better solution is to put on loud music and then chant your ritual at a slightly lower volume. Your housemates might be annoyed by the music, but they won't hear the ritual.

A dark, quiet, calm and atmospheric house will get you in the right state of mind, but if you have to work in a noisy bedroom, it's better than sneaking and whispering. But if whispering is your only option it's better than nothing. (It's been over twenty years since I had housemates, but I remember the problem well, so if this applies to you, I know what you're going through. For many readers, they will be hiding from a spouse when they do a ritual. It's a similar situation, but there are always ways.)

There are lots of different ways to get into the mood and create an atmosphere appropriate for magick, but the advice about settling out of normality remains, whatever your approach. Switch off the devices. Cut off from people. Be alone, be quiet, and shut up and shut down for once – the world is too damned busy and information-laden, and you can't connect with magick if you're in the middle of social media and endless video streaming.

The magickal equipment is minimal. What I do is get two candles; one black, one white. The white one is used to give me some light in the darkened room, so I don't stumble when trying to find the light switch, as well as signaling the beginning and end of the ritual. The black candle is for the ritual burning.

During the ritual, you write down some words on a small piece of paper, and your paper is burned in the black candle's flame. Simple stuff, but worth doing. If you can't get a black candle, use a white one – it's better than nothing. If you can't get a candle, use a lighter. If you can't burn things in your house, for whatever reason, then just tear the paper up instead of burning it. Every compromise *is* a compromise and makes the magick less intoxicating for you, so if you can go out and buy a perfectly black candle, and burn the paper, do that. If you don't want to do any of this, you can simplify the ritual down to nothing but the basic chants, words, the moods and sigils, without any equipment at all. It's not great, but if you're traveling or really unable to do the full working, it does have an effect.

It gets boring saying this, but most occultists say it these days, so forgive me for the public information warning (it's so uncool, I know), but if you mess about with candles and burning scraps of paper, you can burn your house down and then your ritual looks pretty stupid. Candles and burning scraps of paper are deadly. Oh yeah, candles are charming in movies when placed all around the bathtub, and they're great for magick, but if you leave a candle burning or drop the paper that you just ignited, you can quickly get into trouble and your home will burn down around your suffocated corpse. You're not stupid, I know, but some people *really are* – so I have to say this. Take every reasonable and sensible precaution to avoid an accident. If I say 'burn that paper' it means you need to use your brain, and make sure you don't get burnt, and don't drop it on the carpet, and that your candle is secured in a place where it can't fall over and set things on fire. You get the picture. Don't use flames when drunk or high. Sounds so lame in a big bad book of dark magick, but there's nothing quite as lame as setting yourself on fire through being an idiot. Look, it's no more dangerous than a drunken teenager burning incense and falling asleep – that can be deadly too, so I hear. The truth is, if you want to do this safely, you should be surrounded by buckets of water and fire extinguishers, and you should hold the paper with some sort of device to ensure you're safe. That's what you *should* do. I'll let you know what I do. I hold the paper in my hand and when my fingers are about to get burned I drop the very last fragment over the candle and let it ignite. The ashes fall, in very small amounts, around the candle. But that's risky. You burn your fingers quite often. How safe you want to be – that's your choice.

Why do we burn things and bury and spread things that we use in rituals? Do the demons care? No, they don't care, but there's a potency in archetypes and images, and every act is a magickal act once you're in a ritual state. Everything that you create in a ritual becomes more magickal than when it was just something hanging around in your apartment. If you can't get into this part of the magick, you're going to have a tough time getting results. Build the atmosphere. Know that lighting that candle is a signal, a moment where you open up to magick. The flame transforms the candle. The black is a sign of your willingness to work with dark forces. You are calling to demons, and working with symbols of light and darkness.

In each ritual, you burn a piece of paper. You can use any old paper, but here's an optional idea. Have you ever seen that thing kids do, where they wet paper with tea-stained water, and it dries unevenly and looks like parchment? Ok, that's pretty cool if you're six years old, but what's great about this paper is that it doesn't just look old-fashioned a mystical – it goes sort of crisp, and burns fast and gives off an earthier stench. You can use any old office paper dragged out of your printer's tray – that's ok. But if you can be bothered taking this extra step, it's a worthwhile touch. You boil water, make some tea (without milk), and pour the tea over the paper, hang it up to dry, and when it's thoroughly dry you have your crispy parchment. Burns beautifully.

In each ritual, you write your statement on a circle of paper, so you will need to prepare one or more of these in advance. I don't think you need instructions for that, other than, draw a circle that's roughly the size of an inverted coffee mug (that's what I use to draw my outline), and then cut it out. It's just a paper circle at this point, so you don't need to get too exact or excited. Just cut out a circle of paper and you're ready to get started.

Each ritual is performed once only, unless you obtain evidence that you need to perform it again at a later date. Trust the magick and it grows in strength over the coming days and weeks, so do not *look* for evidence that it has failed, or that things have changed to weaken your position. In theory, and in (most) practice, performing the ritual just once, ever, is all you need to cloak a situation in secrecy. Be aware, though, that if you change things in the real world, you may need to add more magick.

You may want to bury something in your garden, and you don't want to be seen. Doesn't matter what it is. You perform a ritual **To Reduce Perception of Your Actions**, employing Carnesiel and Camuel. This means that if anybody should come near you while you are burying your 'treasure,' they will not see you. Their perception of what you are doing will be dampened, and you will remain effectively cloaked. If at a later date, however, you bury something else nearby, or add something to the box (or hole, or whatever you've dug), this is a separate action and situation, so an additional ritual will be required.

If you're having an affair that's hidden being by magick, and you move from occasional meetings in a hotel room to wandering around in a public park, you have changed the nature of the situation, and you will need to add more magick.

The magick works when performed once, but only for the situation it has been applied to. When you change the situation, add more magick. If you understand this paragraph, the magick will work for you.

You will find that for most situations, a single ritual keeps your secret for life. When dealing with enemies, or using the magick in more fluid situations, you may need a sequence of magickal effects to achieve what you desire, with constant adaptation as the situation changes and your enemy changes tactics. You will know when and how to use the magick, by monitoring the situation.

You can try to limit the amount of magick you have to perform by making your initial request more general. 'Hide my affair from everybody, for all time.' Sometimes, though, such general requests feel too outrageous, and it is difficult to put your faith into the ritual, and it is weakened by your doubt. Be guided by your real need. What do you earnestly and sincerely want to hide? When you know that, you know how to guide the magick. Ask for your need to be met, and the ritual will work even if it is quite a general request.

You can perform more than one ritual on one day, but I only recommend this if you are seriously pressed for time, or if you only get one rare opportunity to work in privacy. Otherwise, wait a few days between rituals, to ensure they are given your full energy and attention.

The Ritual

When you want to perform the ritual, have everything you need to hand. A pen or pencil. The small circle of paper you will write on and then burn. A notebook, or sheet of paper, where you make notes for the ritual. Your candles and any holders they are to be placed in. This book. Something to light the candles with. Privacy.

The opening of the ritual involves lighting one candle and writing a short statement about what it is that you want to conceal, but you can prepare for this quite generally for some time in advance. You can think about this and work it over in your mind for hours, days or weeks. Your final thoughts, and the written summary, should occur during the ritual itself. Do not go into a magick ritual with a confused mind. Know what you want, clearly, but not *quite* to the point where you have it refined down to a single sentence. Think this over, know what you want. If this pre-ritual preparation only takes minutes, it only takes minutes, but if you need a week or more to be certain about what you want to conceal, take that time.

To illustrate the following instructions, we will assume that you are working with Pamersiel under Carnesiel **To Hide the Past**. You have started a new relationship, and you don't believe your new partner would understand certain aspects of your violent past, even though you have reformed. You know that you already appear trustworthy, so you don't need the ritual to appear more trustworthy. This ritual has been chosen to keep the past hidden. You spend a few minutes, during one day, thinking about this, and then you know you are ready. Here's what you do:

When you are ready, move to the space where you will perform your magick. I sit at a table, because it's practical and I don't believe that kneeling is the ideal posture when working with demons. You are free to stand by a table or other working surface.

Light your white candle. (It's best if all other lights are now turned off, so long as you can do that safely.) Now make written notes about what it is that you want to achieve. You are trying to summarize your desire, and you're trying to get it down to one sentence. You are not writing an essay, but putting down ideas – you can write scattered thoughts, words, ideas, whole paragraphs; just do what works for you. If you find that a single sentence comes to you immediately, write it down. If not, put in some work until you get there. There is something about sitting in thought and writing that is an authentic process of magick. You are moving from thought to movement to an incarnation of your thought in the written code of language. Yes, it's just your own thoughts written down, but this is still a code, a key to the thoughts you have worked on.

The phrase you are trying to get to is a single sentence, written in the present tense that accurately summarizes the magickal result you want, as though it has already happened.

In this example, you may write, 'My violent past is forever hidden from Marcy.' Earlier, I said magick that is too general can be weak, so is it OK to write 'forever'? Yes, because you are only covering your violent past, not your entire history. If you write, 'Everything about the past ten years is completely hidden from Marcy,' that might be too general.

Your statement must be written in the present tense, as though it's worked already. Never write, 'I hope that my past remains hidden.' The demon takes these statements and makes them real, and you do not want to make your *hope more real*. Imagine time has passed, the magick has worked. How would you summarize it?

I told you to sit with a piece of paper and work this out, but I also noted that you could write it out in one go. How this works out will be different for every person, every time. Sometimes you may struggle to find what it is that you want to say, what it is that you want to achieve. If it feels too difficult, snuff out the candle and try again another time. If you get clarity, write it out, and know that it is your final statement of intent. This is what you will present to the Demon of Adjuration, and the demon will take your written reality and make it real. Now light the black candle, and then write your statement around the outer edge of your circle of paper. It will look something like this:

My violent past is forever hidden from Marich.

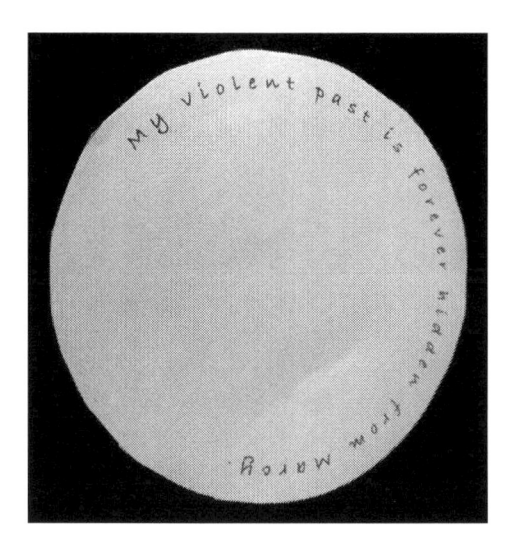

The text doesn't have to go all the way around. If you mess up, or feel it's not right, screw it up and start again. But it doesn't have to be perfect. (Use your own handwriting. I used computer-type because I'd rather keep my handwriting private.)

When you have a circle of paper you are satisfied with, place the paper circle face-down on the table before the black candle, so that the text is *not* seen by you.

Scan your eyes over the seals in the first sigil. This sigil contains the seal of the Emperor Demon and seven subordinate demons. Scanning is a way of looking that is not the same as staring, but is more than a passing glance. It's nothing complicated – all you do is look at the demonic seal for a few seconds. What's important is not how you look, but that as you do, you know that it is more than a set of lines. It is a demonic signature. Know that it is a key to contact. Know that letting the image into your mind invites the demon to know you.

In this example, you will start by scanning the sigil of Carnesiel (in the central circle). After a few seconds, move to Orich on the top right, and continue the scan until you reach
Vadriel on the top left. You do not need to know the demon names as you scan the seals. You do not need to stare for minutes. A few seconds is all you need, at most, for each seal. And remember, scanning is easy; I could say 'look at the sigil,' but that makes it sound like you're meant to study and understand it. The word 'scan' implies that you let the shapes sink into you, that you look at them

with the same sort of feeling you would have when viewing abstract art. You're not trying to understand or to see anything. You only need to see the sigil, and know that it opens your mind to demonic contact.

When you have scanned all eight seals in the first sigil, gaze at the flame of the black candle. As you gaze at the flame, chant the name of the Emperor Demon for your chosen ritual. In this ritual, the Emperor Demon is Carnesiel. (In each ritual, you are clearly told the name of the Emperor Demon, so you know what to say. Also, it is the very first name written underneath the first sigil. You can't miss it. The pronunciation is written in bold letters – just say these sounds as though they are English and you'll get it right. If you get it slightly wrong, it doesn't matter, because the demonic seals do most of the work. Do note, however, that G always sounds like the G in GET rather than the G in GEM).

You chant the name Carnesiel until you feel a change in the atmosphere. It might happen the moment you open your mouth, or it might take five minutes, but if you gaze at the candle flame and chant the name over and over, you will, at some point, feel a magickal change. Do not expect a huge change. You might get a big effect – such as a rush of cool air, or heat in your skin, or a roaring in your ears. But it's more likely you'll get a mild shiver down the spine, or perhaps something even less dramatic, like the slightest feeling of the supernatural. If you feel *anything*, other than normal, that's a success.

If it doesn't work at all, and you sense no change whatsoever, the bad news is that it's wiser to stop and try again at another time, when your mind is clear of expectations, when you are relaxed, and when you are able to connect to magick. It may take a few attempts. It usually works immediately. Expect success, and remember, the smallest shiver *is* success – it means contact has been made. Don't sit there thinking, 'I wonder if that slightly dizzy feeling I have is the demon, or if it would have happened anyway.' *Anything* that is different to normal *is* demonic contact. At this point, stop chanting, and know that contact has been made.

Now speak the names of the remaining demons from the first sigil, once each. If you've learned them, you can gaze at the flame as you do this, but if you need to read them, they are written beneath the name of the Emperor Demon. Say each name once, and as you say it, know you're calling for that demon's attention. You are commanding it to join the ritual. This sense of knowing is very important, and more important than how you say the names.

Turn your attention to the second sigil. Scan your eyes over the seal of the Demon of Adjuration and say the demon's name three times, knowing that the demon cannot ignore you. In this example, you would say Pamersiel three times. The Demon of Adjuration is always the first-listed name beneath the second sigil.

Now take your circle of paper, and place it on your left palm, face up, so that you can see the text. You don't need to read the text; it just needs to be that way up. Feel what it is that you want to achieve, but feel it as though your desire has been granted. Enjoy the satisfaction of knowing that your desire is already real. As soon as you manage to imagine how it would feel to get your wish, however fleetingly, take the paper in either hand (or use an implement of your choice), and touch it to the black candle's flame. Know that as it burns, your command is being made real by the demon.

You may wish to light the paper and then place it in a metal bowl, or somewhere else, so that it can burn to ashes in a contained way. Or you may keep hold of it as I do, dropping the final fragment into the flame at the last moment – this can lead to you extinguishing the candle or burning yourself. It always leads to the ash falling all around the candle. If there are any unburned scraps of paper left, do not be concerned, but place them back into the flame until everything has turned to ash.

As soon as the last of the paper has turned to ash, scan your eyes over the remaining demonic seals in the sigil. Start on the top right, and scan clockwise, until you reach the last seal. As soon as this is done, you speak the names of the demons. In this example, the seven names a printed directly below Pamersiel, and you would start with Anoyr and end with Madres. These demonic names are said quite dispassionately. All you need to know is that they are servants of the Demon of Adjuration, and they are being called to work the magick for you.

After you have spoken the final name, gaze at the black candle flame, and by way of thanks say the name of the Demon of Adjuration, and then the Demon Emperor, and the work is done. You only need to do this as an act of thanks. There is no need to drum up the feeling of great gratitude. The demon has been called to work for you, and will.

Extinguish the black candle, then the white. (You may wish to turn the lights on before putting out the white candle., to avoid stumbling around in a dark and recently demon-filled room.)

You should now return to normal, and there's no better way to do that than to clear up your ritual mess. Wiping up bits of ash, washing your hands, hiding your occult equipment – it all brings you back down to earth. The objects are now just objects. The ash is just dirt, and nothing magickal. Make it feel like an ordinary mess that you are clearing up.

Forget about the ritual. The magick may begin to work immediately, or may build up its power over the coming days.

The ritual may sound complicated, but it is not, and if you read it carefully a few times, you will find that the process is simple. Once you are familiar with it, you can use the following summary.

To perform the ritual, you do this:

Spend some time deciding what it is you want, and which ritual you will use.

Prepare your equipment. Spend an hour settling down, away from ordinary distractions. Go to the place where you intend to work.

Light your candle and make notes about the result you want. Condense this down to a present-tense statement.

Light the black candle and write your statement around the outer edge of your paper circle. Place the paper circle face-down on the table before the black candle.

Scan your eyes over the first sigil, as detailed in the instructions.

Gaze at the flame of the black candle. As you gaze at the flame, chant the name of the Emperor Demon for your chosen ritual, until you feel a change in the atmosphere.

Speak the names of the remaining demons from the first sigil, and know you are calling them into the ritual.

Turn your attention to the second sigil. Scan your eyes over the central seal, as instructed. Speak the name of the Demon of

Adjuration.

Place the circle of paper on your left palm, face up. Feel what it is that you want to achieve, as though it has been achieved. Burn the paper in the candle flame. Speak the names of the remaining seven demons.

Gaze at the flame, and by way of thanks, say the name of the Demon of Adjuration once more, and then speak the name of the Demon Emperor, and know the work is done.

Extinguish the black candle, then the white.

Return to normal.

The Veil of Secrecy

The Veil of Secrecy is governed by Carnesiel of the East, who has power over the demons Pamersiel, Padiel, Camuel and Aschiel. The four powers of the veil can be employed as follows:

To hide the past, employ Carnesiel and Pamersiel. Hide what you did in the past. Hide anything that you do not want to emerge.

To reduce personal suspicion, employ Carnesiel and Padiel. Hide an action you are involved in by reducing suspicion in a specific person.

To reduce perception of your actions, employ Carnesiel and Camuel. Hide an action you are involved in, by dampening perceptions regarding that action.

To bring silence, employ Carnesiel and Aschiel. Make others who are involved in an action, or who know of your past, remain silent.

To Hide the Past

Pamersiel under Carnesiel

When you wish to hide something that you have done, an incident you were involved in, or an entire area of your life from the past, this is the ritual you use. It is highly adaptable, and can be used to cast a general cloak of concealment over a period of time, or an incident. It can also be used quite specifically, to hide a particular past event or period of time from a certain person. As always, be guided by your actual need when crafting your request.

As an example, if you spent time in prison, and want that time in your life to remain hidden, you could use this ritual to hide it from everybody in your future. This will, of course, require you to put in a great deal of work yourself. As with all magick, you don't rely on the magick entirely, but let it empower your own efforts, and add supernatural effects to your natural caution.

A second example could be the classic extramarital affair. It's over, and now you want it to remain hidden. If you wish for it to remain hidden from all, including your close friends, that is possible. But perhaps you only wish it to remain hidden from your partner, so that it is something you *can* discuss with friends. Consider carefully before choosing.

The past you try to hide can be as recent as an hour ago, or something that occurred many years before. It may be a moment you wish to hide, or an entire period of your life. Although this ritual will obscure the past, it may not silence others, and in such cases, should be used in combination with other rituals, to silence those who may be tempted to speak out.

The opening chant is made to the Emperor Demon Carnesiel (CAR-NESS-EE-ELL). The request is spoken to the Demon of Adjuration Pamersiel (PAM-AIR-SEE-ELL).

Carnesiel (CAR-NESS-EE-ELL)

Orich (OH-RICK)
Zabriel (ZAB-REE-ELL)
Buchafas (BUCK-AFF-ASS)
Arisiel (ARISS-EE-ELL)
Bedary (BED-ARE-EE)
Laphor (LAFF-OAR)
Vadriel (VADD-REE-ELL)

Pamersiel (PAM-AIR-SEE-ELL)

Anoyr (AN-AWE-EAR)
Madriel (MAD-REE-ELL)
Ebras (EBB-RAZ)
Ormenus (OAR-MEN-UZ)
Rablion (RAB-LEE-ON)
Abrulges (AB-RULL-GEZ)
Madres (MAD-REZ)

To Reduce Personal Suspicion

Padiel under Carnesiel

When you wish to hide something that is currently taking place, you can use this ritual to conceal it from a named individual. This only works when you know the person in question, and when you work the ritual on one person at a time. It is not for general concealment, but will prevent one individual from becoming suspicious about a particular activity.

If you're trying to take over a business by undermining various people, this ritual would not be useful. If, however, you were only undermining one person, by diverse acts, this ritual could hide those acts. If you are committing adultery or other personal indiscretions, you can make the one person who *might* be suspicious, lose their suspicion. If you come home tainted with evidence, or if your lifestyle pattern changes in a way that *should* be suspicious, or if you act defensively when you shouldn't, this ritual can cover up the glaringly obvious. You should, of course, remain cautious, but for any activity, the ritual will make one person lose the ability to see that what you are doing is out of place.

When writing your statement, summarize the situation or action you are hiding, and name the person you are hiding this action from.

You will note that, unusually, the sigil of Padiel contains only one seal – the seal of Padiel. There are no subordinate demons. This is because, in the grimoires, they are not named, as it was deemed unnecessary, and assumed that Padiel has the power to source and control the required demons at will. When the paper turns to ash, there is no further visual scan. Instead, move straight to the thanks and closing of the ritual.

The opening chant is made to the Emperor Demon Carnesiel (CAR-NESS-EE-ELL). The request is spoken to the Demon of Adjuration Padiel (PAD-EE-ELL).

Carnesiel (CAR-NESS-EE-ELL)

Buchafas (BUCK-AFF-ASS)
Armany (ARM-AN-EE)
Arisiel (ARISS-EE-ELL)
Capriel (CAP-REE-ELL)
Bedary (BED-ARE-EE)
Zabriel (ZAB-REE-ELL)
Laphor (LAFF-OAR)

Padiel (PAD-EE-ELL)

To Reduce Perception of Your Actions

Camuel under Carnesiel

When you are involved in activities that should remain hidden from all, except those you invite into your confidence, use this ritual. It will conceal all your actions and activities, within reason, related to the action you define. This is similar to the preceding ritual, except that you are able to cast a cloak of secrecy that affects all who may perceive what it is that you are doing.

Be careful not to conceal aspects of your work that you want to be visible. Imagine you are a creator of fine diamond rings, and there is some aspect of your business that needs to remain secret. You do not want to make your entire business secret, otherwise it will stop being seen by people. Your clients and customers will barely know you exist. Direct the effect of the ritual only at the aspect of the business that needs to be hidden.

There is no need to specify who the activity should be hidden from, as it will become generally cloaked, and will only be seen by those who are shown it deliberately.

In case it isn't already obvious, this does not apply only to business, but to any action you are currently involved in. For example, I've known it to be used by public figures who have hidden (and extreme) sex lives.

Should there be a substantial change in the nature or intensity of the actions you are hiding, you will be required to repeat the ritual, with an expanded definition.

The opening chant is made to the Emperor Demon Carnesiel (CAR-NESS-EE-ELL). The request is spoken to the Demon of Adjuration Camuel (CAM-OO-ELL).

Carnesiel (CAR-NESS-EE-ELL)

Cumeriel (COO-MEH-REE-ELL)
Capriel (CAP-REE-ELL)
Bedary (BED-ARE-EE)
Laphor (LAFF-OAR)
Orich (OH-RICK)
Zabriel (ZAB-REE-ELL)
Arisiel (ARISS-EE-ELL)

Camuel (CAM-OO-ELL)

Phaniel (FAR-NEE-ELL)
Pariel (PAH-REE-ELL)
Meras (MEH-RAZ)
Asniel (AZ-NEE-ELL)
Citgara (KIT-GAH-RAH)
Tediel (TED-EE-ELL)
Moriel (MORE-EE-ELL)

To Bring Silence

Aschiel under Carnesiel

When others know your secrets, you need to keep those people as quiet as you are. This ritual can be used to silence those who know about your distant past, as well as those who share your current actions.

If, for example, you performed some secret activity, many years ago, and you become concerned that the truth may come out, you may want to silence a particular individual. This may be because the individual has begun to talk, or it may be because you have simply become afraid, even though there is no actual evidence that the other person will share your secrets.

If you and several associates are working on something that needs to be hidden – whether it's software technology that could be stolen by a competitor, or something more obscure - there are many reasons you may need to silence those you work with. It could be that you worry they will betray you deliberately or by accident. This ritual will help to bring silence upon them, so that they keep secrets as well as you do.

If you need to name several people, you may find that you have to write around the circle of paper more than once, and that your writing spirals in toward the center of the circle. That is ok. It is better to name everybody than to just name the group.

The opening chant is made to the Emperor Demon Carnesiel (CAR-NESS-EE-ELL). The request is spoken to the Demon of Adjuration Aschiel (ASK-EE-ELL).

Carnesiel (CAR-NESS-EE-ELL)

Bedary (BED-ARE-EE)
Capriel (CAP-REE-ELL)
Cumeriel (COO-MEH-REE-ELL)
Vadriel (VADD-REE-ELL)
Zabriel (ZAB-REE-ELL)
Buchafas (BUCK-AFF-ASS)
Arisiel (ARISS-EE-ELL)

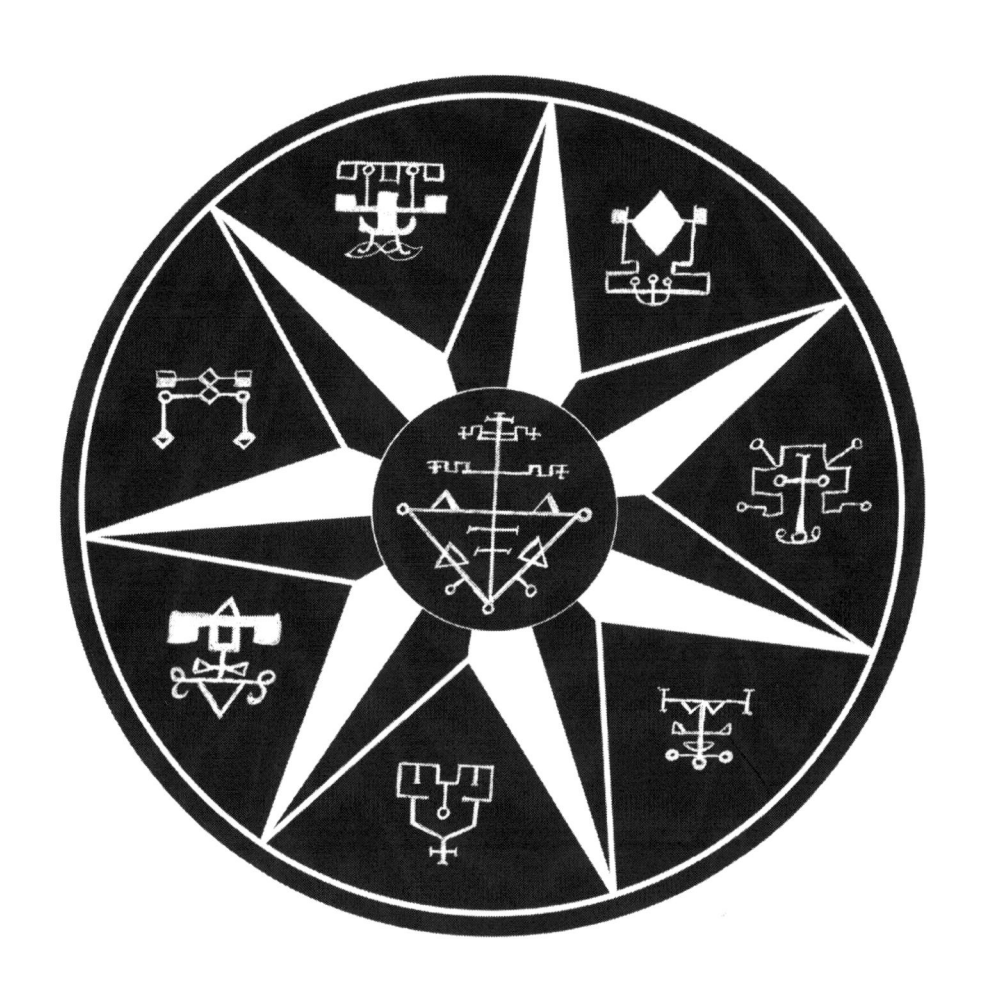

Aschiel (ASK-EE-ELL)

Othiel (OTH-EE-ELL)
Asphiel (AZ-FEE-ELL)
Bufar (BOO-FAR)
Melos (MEL-OZ)
Curiel (COO-REE-ELL)
Chamos (KAM-OSS)
Odiel (AWE-DEE-ELL)

The Shadow of False Beliefs

The Shadow of False Beliefs is governed by Caspiel of the South, who has power over the demons Barmiel, Gediel, Asyriel and Maseriel. The four powers of the shadow can be employed as follows:

To appear plausible, employ Caspiel and Barmiel. Make something you claim seem generally plausible.

To appear trustworthy, employ Caspiel and Gediel. Influence people to believe you are a trustworthy person.

To encourage false beliefs, employ Caspiel and Asyriel. Let a false belief arise within the mind of another, without you saying anything.

To seem believable under scrutiny, employ Caspiel and Maseriel. Make those who observe and question you closely believe that you are trustworthy.

To Appear Plausible

Barmiel under Caspiel

Whether you're selling yourself, your personality, a product, or a business, you are *selling*. You are always trying to sell a version of yourself to somebody, and that requires the appearance of plausibility. Do you appear genuine, like you really know what you're saying, or does everybody sense that you're a fraud? The sad truth is that some people seem like weak, implausible deceivers even when they are genuine. Others, who lie skillfully, appear to be the most plausible and wise. Whether truthful or deceiver, you should *appear* plausible, or your power is diminished. This applies at home, work, in business or in any area of life.

You can use this ritual to give yourself an overall air and appearance of plausibility. You can also aim the ritual at a specific situation or person. You may wish for your plausibility to improve in a business situation, in a relationship, in one particular place or during one set time. You can do both; give yourself a general air of plausibility and then repeat the ritual when you want to aim it at a specific situation. A general air of plausibility will work, but remember that more direct magick, aimed at a specific area, can be more potent, so the combination is often best.

The opening chant is made to the Emperor Demon Caspiel (CASS-PEA-ELL). The request is spoken to the Demon of Adjuration Barmiel (BAR-ME-ELL).

Caspiel (CASS-PEA-ELL)

Otiel (OAT-EE-ELL)
Ambri (AM-BREE)
Usiel (OO-SEE-ELL)
Chariel (CAR-EE-ELL)
Femel (FEM-ELL)
Camori (CAM-OAR-EE)
Larmol (LAR-MOLL)

Barmiel (BAR-ME-ELL)

Mansi (MAN-SEE)
Barbis (BAR-BEEZ)
Carpiel (CAR-PEA-ELL)
Morcaza (MORE-CAH-ZA)
Caniel (CAR-NEE-ELL)
Keriel (KEH-REE-ELL)
Baabal (BAH-AH-BAHL)

To Appear Trustworthy

Gediel under Caspiel

If this sounds the same as the ritual for plausibility, you've missed the point. Appearing plausible means that people generally assume you are somebody who tells the truth, who knows what is being said, who listens, and has wisdom, knowledge and understanding. When you appear trustworthy, you make yourself appear as though you are somebody that can actually be trusted. Trusted with money, with secret information, and with countless other situations that give you power.

You will often find yourself in situations where your progress stalls because the other person does not trust you. You might be trying to make a deal, start a relationship, sell an idea or just make a sale – if you aren't trusted, you don't make progress.

Like the last ritual, this one can be used to give you an overall air and atmosphere of trustworthiness. This improves the chances of you being seen as trustworthy. And then, if at any point you know there is a specific person, group or situation where more trust is required, you can target it in advance, or when you see a problem arise.

The opening chant is made to the Emperor Demon Caspiel (CASS-PEA-ELL). The request is spoken to the Demon of Adjuration Gediel (GED-EE-ELL).

Caspiel (CASS-PEA-ELL)

Geriel (GEH-REE-ELL)
Aridiel (AH-REED-EE-ELL)
Camori (CAM-OAR-EE)
Femel (FEM-ELL)
Chariel (CAR-EE-ELL)
Ambri (AM-BREE)
Budarym (BOO-DAH-REEM)

Gediel (GED-EE-ELL)

Reciel (REH-SEE-ELL)
Aroan (AH-RAW-AN)
Aglas (AH-GLAHZ)
Cirecas (KEY-RECK-AZ)
Vriel (VREE-ELL)
Anael (ANNE-AH-ELL)
Sadiel (SAH-DEE-ELL)

To Encourage False Beliefs

Asyriel under Caspiel

Convincing somebody of something, when it's absolutely false, can be easy, difficult or a gamble. If you speak a falsehood, you may actually reveal the lie, because you are not lying well enough. A subtler, more powerful and cunning way to change minds is to make people form an idea, and think it is their own. You infiltrate their consciousness and make them come to believe something.

The ability to have thoughts arise within another is truly spectacular, of course, but it should be made clear that this specific ritual works best for false beliefs. If you're trying to convince somebody of the truth, then work on appearing plausible and trustworthy. But when you want somebody to believe something false, something that is absolutely untrue, perform this ritual.

Be very clear in your own mind what it is you want the person to believe. You may want a person to believe they are loved or hated by another. You may want a competitor to believe in something that is actually a time-wasting distraction. You may want a family member to believe you are working for the best of everybody. The power of falsehood, arising within another, is truly great. This power, when used with creative flair, is possibly the most powerful in the book. The belief may grow slowly, or appear instantly, and there's no way of urging the process along. The power is worthy of your patience.

The opening chant is made to the Emperor Demon Caspiel (CASS-PEA-ELL). The request is spoken to the Demon of Adjuration Asyriel (AZ-EAR-EE-ELL).

Caspiel (CASS-PEA-ELL)

Larmol (LAR-MOLL)
Aridiel (AH-REED-EE-ELL)
Geriel (GEH-REE-ELL)
Budarym (BOO-DAH-REEM)
Maras (MAR-AZ)
Otiel (OAT-EE-ELL)
Ambri (AM-BREE)

Asyriel (AZ-EAR-EE-ELL)

Cusiel (COO-SEE-ELL)
Fascua (FASS-QUEUE-AH)
Budar (BOO-DAH)
Maroth (MA-WRATH)
Amiel (AM-EE-ELL)
Aspiel (AZ-PEA-ELL)
Onuel (AWE-NOO-ELL)

To Seem Believable Under Scrutiny

Maseriel under Caspiel

When you have brought about deception, or simply performed an act that should remain hidden, you may come under great scrutiny. This might be a court case where you're innocent (or not so innocent), an interrogation from a spouse or partner, an investigation by your boss, or even just unwanted questioning from a friend who suspects you're up to no good.

As soon as you know that somebody is going to question you, perform this ritual. You do not need to name the individual who may be the one questioning you. Instead, aim the ritual at the situation you are being questioned about, and your ability to remain believable when scrutinized. The ritual was structured this way because you often have no idea exactly who will be questioning you. So even if you have a court case coming up, you don't aim this at the judge; you let the demon know that you want to appear truthful when you are scrutinized about your situation – whatever that situation may be.

Even when answering difficult questions and giving false answers, you will appear believable. The ritual works by giving you a skilled silver tongue, as well as making those who hear you talk about this subject feel that your words are believable.

The opening chant is made to the Emperor Demon Caspiel (CASS-PEA-ELL). The request is spoken to the Demon of Adjuration Maseriel (MAZ-AIR-EE-ELL).

Caspiel (CASS-PEA-ELL)

Larmol (LAR-MOLL)
Geriel (GEH-REE-ELL)
Camori (CAM-OAR-EE)
Ambri (AM-BREE)
Maras (MAR-AZ)
Aridiel (AH-REED-EE-ELL)
Usiel (OO-SEE-ELL)

Maseriel (MAZ-AIR-EE-ELL)

Earos (EE-AH-ROSS)
Rabiel (RAH-BEE-ELL)
Solvar (SAUL-VAH)
Patiel (PAH-TEA-ELL)
Maras (MAH-RAZ)
Eliel (ELL-EE-ELL)
Badiel (BAH-DEE-ELL)

The Flame of Confusion

The Flame of Confusion is governed by Amenadiel of the West, who has power over the demons Malgaras, Dorochiel, Usiel and Cabariel. The four powers of the flame can be employed as follows:

To confuse an individual, employ Amenadiel and Malgaras. You can make a specific individual confused about a subject.

To bring general confusion, employ Amenadiel and Dorochiel. Bring general confusion to perceptions about an event.

To discourage clarity of thought, employ Amenadiel and Usiel. Make an individual find it difficult to understand what you have done.

To encourage forgetfulness, employ Amenadiel and Cabariel. Make people extremely forgetful about an event.

To Confuse an Individual

Malgaras under Amenadiel

Never underestimate the power of confusion. Have you ever seen a busy parent with three young kids trying to sort out the taxes? Or somebody who's late to the airport in a foreign country trying to work out how much to pay the cab driver? When you're under pressure, feeling confused and overwhelmed, you can't think straight. You don't see the obvious. This makes it very difficult to see through deception. Use confusion to build up this foggy pressure, so that the person you target is unable to see things clearly, and cannot see a situation that you choose to hide. Aim this at one person. (If you need to confuse a group, use the next ritual.)

Be careful about when and where you use this. Do you really want your boss so confused that the business you work for is badly damaged? But if somebody appears aware of your secrets, and you need to stop them finding out more, a dose of confusion could make the trail go cold.

The purpose of the ritual is to make an individual confused about a specific subject, or an area of your life. But be aware that the individual may be plagued by a general level of confusion, especially if they are really trying to focus on the subject you're hiding. You may reserve this magick for people who are not as close to you as your partner or boss.

Although the effects of this ritual could theoretically last a lifetime, your need to hide something usually lessens over time, and the confusion of your target is then gradually relaxed.

The opening chant is made to the Emperor Demon Amenadiel (AH-MEN-AH-DEE-ELL). The request is spoken to the Demon of Adjuration Malgaras (MAL-GAR-AZ).

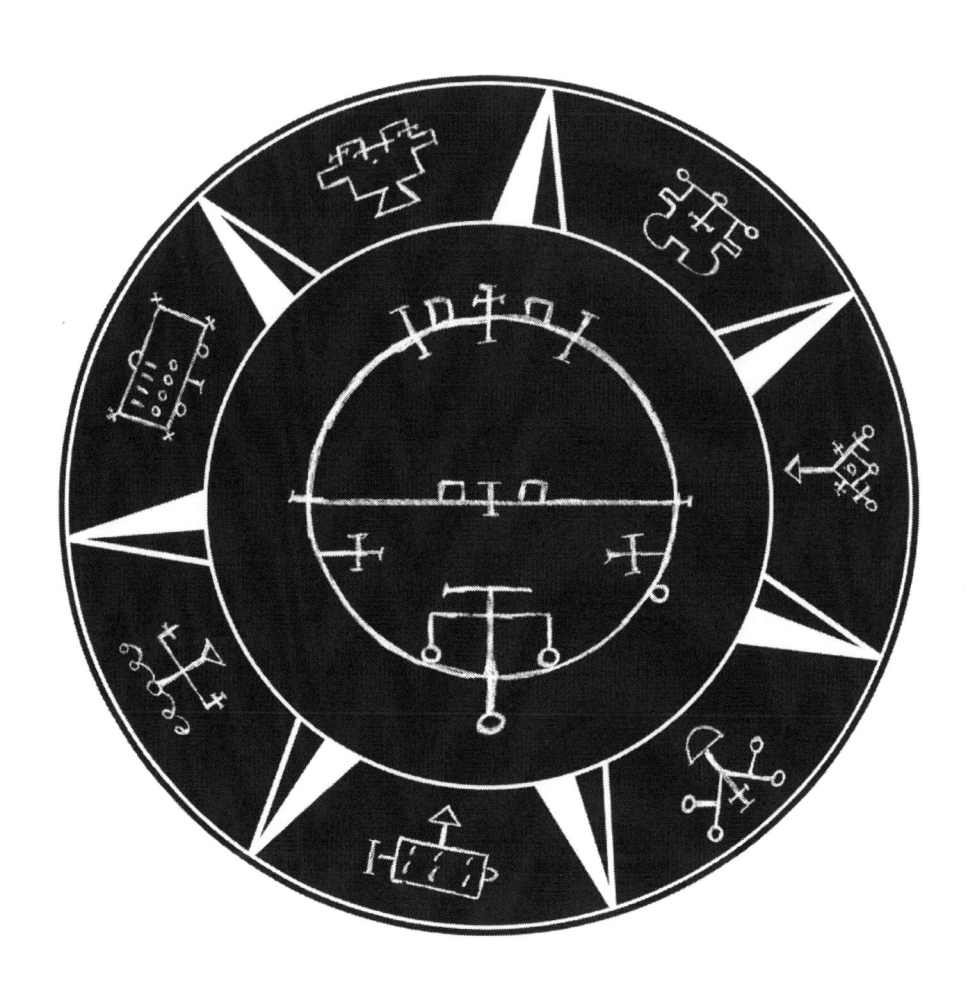

Amenadiel (AH-MEN-AH-DEE-ELL)

Luriel (LOO-REE-ELL)
Almesiel (AL-MEZ-EE-ELL)
Musiriel (MOO-SEE-REE-ELL)
Zoeniel (ZAW-EN-EE-ELL)
Rapsiel (RAP-SEE-ELL)
Curifas (COO-REE-FASS)
Balsur (BAL-SOOR)

Malgaras (MAL-GAR-AZ)

Cubi (COO-BEE)
Libiel (LIB-EE-ELL)
Aspiel (AZ-PEA-ELL)
Basiel (BAZ-EE-ELL)
Aspor (AZ-POUR)
Caron (CAH-RAWN)
Dodiel (DAW-DEE-ELL)

To Bring General Confusion

Dorochiel under Amenadiel

Confusing a group of people sounds like it might cause chaos, but this ritual brings cluttered thoughts regarding a specific subject. It's similar to the previous ritual, but is aimed at a group, and its effects are not quite as disruptive. If there's a group of people that you want to confuse, so they can't think clearly, use this.

You need to think carefully about whether confusion will work for you. If you're going to a group job interview, do you really want to confuse everybody who's interviewing you? Probably not. But if you're doing some secret work that could draw the wrong sort of attention from co-workers, then causing them all to feel confused when they approach this subject – that can work extremely well.

You don't need to name all the individuals in the group, but you need a label for them. It might be, 'Everybody I work with,' or 'All the people in my house.' If it's clear to you, it will be clear to the demon. The subject area you are trying to hide can be quite broad and general, but remember you are not trying to make these people generally confused. You name the situation and you label the group, so that they can never clarify their perceptions about your activities in that specific area.

The opening chant is made to the Emperor Demon Amenadiel (AH-MEN-AH-DEE-ELL). The request is spoken to the Demon of Adjuration Dorochiel (DOOR-AWE-KEY-ELL).

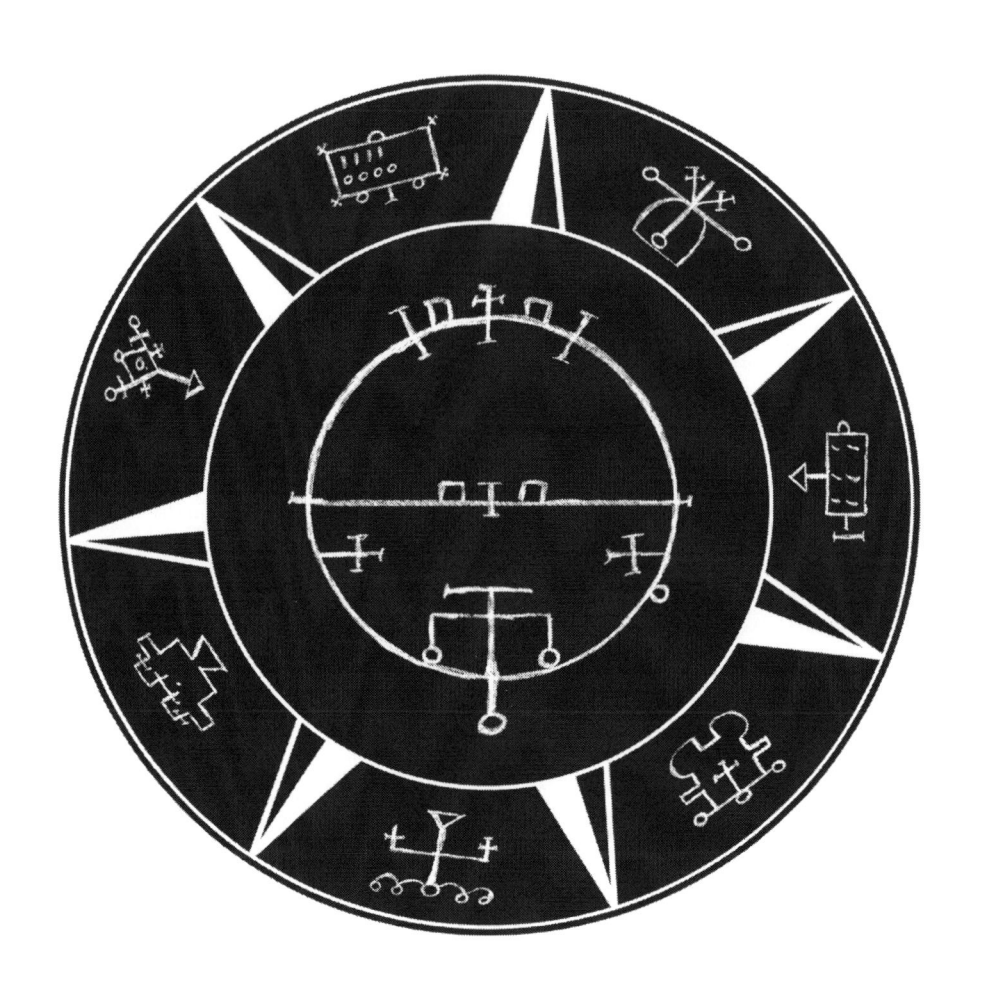

Amenadiel (AH-MEN-AH-DEE-ELL)

Vadras (VAD-RAZ)
Zoeniel (ZAW-EN-EE-ELL)
Luriel (LOO-REE-ELL)
Rapsiel (RAP-SEE-ELL)
Balsur (BAL-SOOR)
Almesiel (AL-MEZ-EE-ELL)
Curifas (COO-REE-FASS)

Dorochiel (DOOR-AWE-KEY-ELL)

Maziel (MAZ-EE-ELL)
Bulis (BOO-LIZ)
Momel (MAW-MELL)
Pasiel (PAZ-EE-ELL)
Vraniel (VRAH-NEE-ELL)
Paniel (PAH-NEE-ELL)
Cadriel (CAD-REE-ELL)

To Discourage Clarity of Thought

Usiel under Amenadiel

Causing confusion can help you to avoid discovery, but when you've been discovered, when you're caught in the act, what then? If somebody has seen what you're up to, you need to discourage clarity of thought around this subject.

You've been caught massaging figures in your favor. Somebody saw you do it – they witnessed you in the act. Or you've been seen with somebody you're not meant to be with. Or you've been heard saying something that makes it clear you've been lying. What now? You need to make this subject or incident something that cannot be perceived clearly.

This works best when only one other person has overheard or discovered you. If there's more than one, name them all and hope for the best, but it does work best when it's just one person. Name the person, and name the situation that has been discovered. This means that whenever the person tries to think about the subject, they will not be able to think clearly. Usually, they will start to think about something else. This can be so powerful that it will leave you dumbfounded. You can be caught in the act, and so long as you use this ritual before the questioning gets too heavy, the person you target will be unable to form any opinion, or any deep suspicions, about what they saw.

The opening chant is made to the Emperor Demon Amenadiel (AH-MEN-AH-DEE-ELL). The request is spoken to the Demon of Adjuration Usiel (OO-SEA-ELL).

Amenadiel (AH-MEN-AH-DEE-ELL)

Camiel (CAM-EE-ELL)
Luriel (LOO-REE-ELL)
Rapsiel (RAP-SEE-ELL)
Zoeniel (ZAW-EN-EE-ELL)
Musiriel (MOO-SEE-REE-ELL)
Balsur (BAL-SOOR)
Almesiel (AL-MEZ-EE-ELL)

Usiel (OO-SEA-ELL)

Saddiel (SAH-DEE-ELL)
Pathir (PATH-EAR)
Ethiel (ETH-EE-ELL)
Ofsidiel (ORF-SID-EE-ELL)
Almoel (AL-MAW-ELL)
Marae (MAR-EYE)
Asuriel (AZ-OO-REE-ELL)

To Encourage Forgetfulness

Cabariel under Amenadiel

This ritual lets you make one person, or a group of people, become forgetful about a specific event or period of time.

Whatever you've done, if it's been seen, known, talked about or in any way perceived, you may want it to be forgotten. It works on recent events, or old stories that have come back to haunt you. The ritual works in two ways. It genuinely makes the memories weak and difficult to hold onto, but it also creates discomfort in those who ponder what they saw or heard.

When designing your ritual, you should name the situation that you wish people to forget, summarizing it clearly but briefly. You can then direct the ritual at one individual, or a specific group. You can even say, 'Anybody who knows this,' if you like, and that can work. If you want to be very thorough, you can perform it three times. The first time, aim it at the most important person that you wish to become forgetful. The second time, aim it at a general group that you would like to let go of the memory. Finally, create a general forgetfulness, so that nobody remembers what went on.

Although this ritual can be extremely disruptive and powerful, it can also bring healing. I helped somebody use this after a wedding that had descended into drunken arguments between several members of the family. With a little work, we were able to make everybody forget. And no, it wasn't alcohol that made them forget. The animosity had continued for days, until we put the ritual to work. They didn't have their memories wiped, but when they look at the wedding photos today, nobody focuses on the arguments that went on that day. It's powerful magick.

The opening chant is made to the Emperor Demon Amenadiel (AH-MEN-AH-DEE-ELL). The request is spoken to the Demon of Adjuration Cabariel (CAB-ARE-EE-ELL).

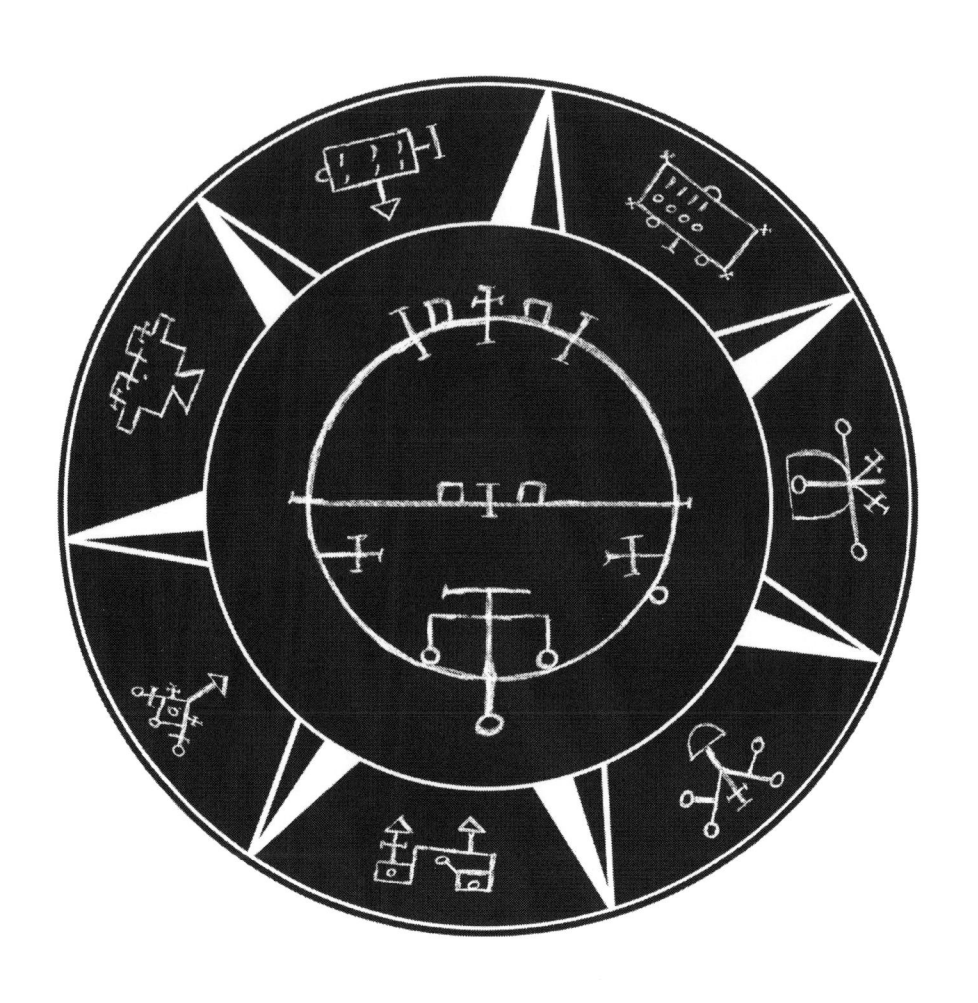

Amenadiel (AH-MEN-AH-DEE-ELL)

Curifas (COO-REE-FASS)
Vadras (VAD-RAZ)
Musiriel (MOO-SEE-REE-ELL)
Lamael (LAH-MAH-ELL)
Almesiel (AL-MEZ-EE-ELL)
Balsur (BAL-SOOR)
Zoeniel (ZAW-EN-EE-ELL)

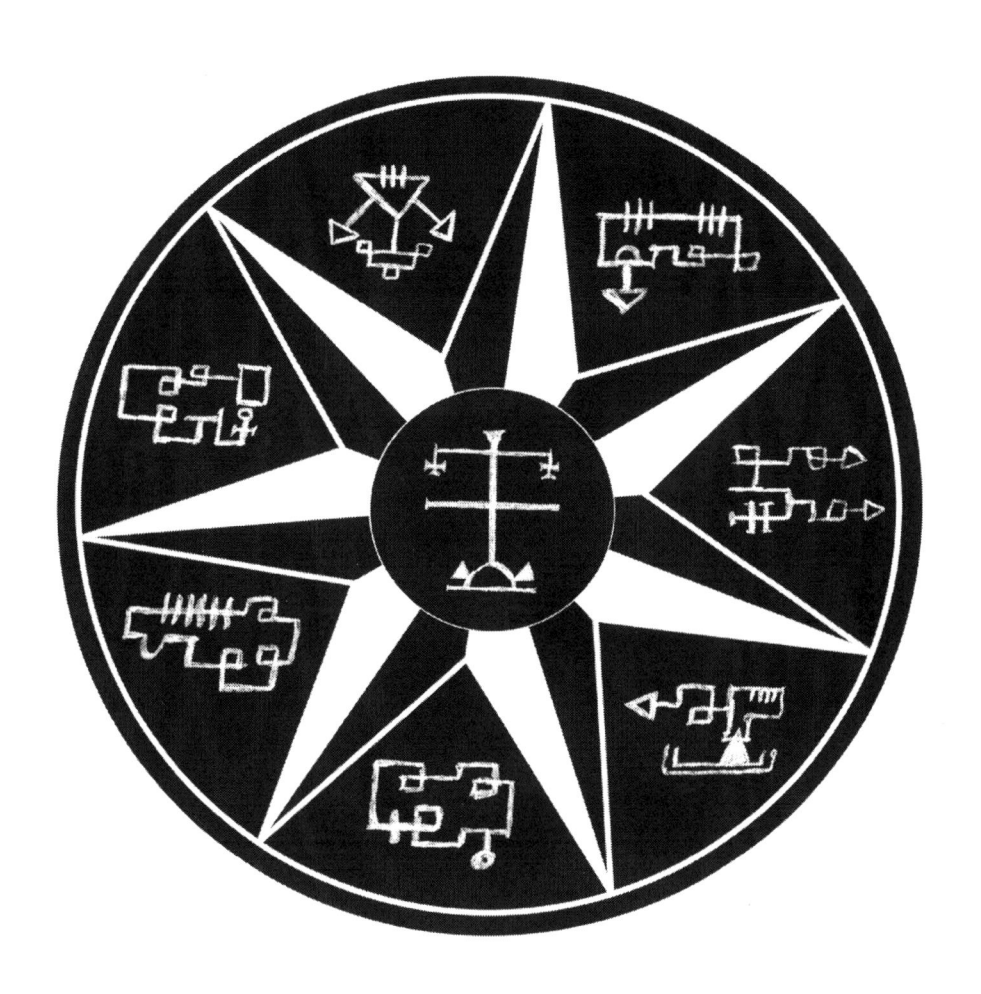

Cabariel (CAB-ARE-EE-ELL)

Mador (MAD-OAR)
Pandor (PAN-DOOR)
Thalbus (THAL-BUZ)
Peniel (PEN-EE-EL)
Orym (AWE-REEM)
Ladiel (LAH-DEE-ELL)
Morias (MORE-EE-AZ)

The Mask of Concealment

The Mask of Concealment is governed by Demoriel of the North, who has power over the demons Rasiel, Symiel, Armadiel and Baruchas. The four powers of the mask can be employed as follows:

To become less visible, employ Demoriel and Rasiel. Become less visible to all, during acts of deception.

To distract attention, employ Demoriel and Symiel. Make those who are near your actions look the other way.

To blur the truth, employ Demoriel and Armadiel. Make people with evidence against you, unable to see or speak the truth.

To move attention to another, employ Demoriel and Baruchas. Direct attention and interest to another person.

To Become Less Visible

Rasiel under Demoriel

Use this ritual before a planned act of deception, to become almost invisible to others. There is no such thing as an 'invisibility spell,' but occultists have long known that there are ways to dampen your own aura, to make your presence seem unimportant, and at the same time to make those who witness you be distracted by other thoughts and images. In many ways, this is almost like being invisible. It does not make you vanish. People will see you! But you will not be seen carrying out the act that you are trying to hide.

You do not aim this at an individual, or even a specific group. The ritual is about you, and making you less visible during a particular period of time. You can aim this at one event – you're planning to go somewhere, do something and you don't want this act to be seen. It might be a five-minute action, or something that lasts more than a day. You can even aim the ritual at something that is going to take several weeks or longer, but when the time is longer, try to be very specific about the act. If, for example, you enter a building every day for a month for a secret reason, and you don't want to be seen, you aren't asking the demon to make you unseen at all times – you ask to be less visible each time you enter and leave that building. Nothing more.

It bears repeating that if you rely on the magick and become too relaxed, you've wasted your time and will be seen. Magick should not let you bring down your guard.

The opening chant is made to the Emperor Demon Demoriel (DEM-OAR-EE-ELL). The request is spoken to the Demon of Adjuration Rasiel (RAH-ZEE-ELL). Although the name sounds the same as the archangel Raziel, they are not the same entity, of course, and the demonic seal ensures there's no confusion.

Demoriel (DEM-OAR-EE-ELL)

Dubilon (DO-BEE-LAWN)
Menador (MEN-ADORE)
Burisiel (BOO-REE-SEE-ELL)
Arnibiel (ARE-NIB-EE-ELL)
Diriel (DEE-REE-ELL)
Medar (MED-ARE)
Carnol (CAR-KNOLL)

Rasiel (RAH-ZEE-ELL)

Morael (MORE-AH-ELL)
Thurcal (THOOR-CAL)
Lamas (LAM-AZ)
Sarach (SAH-RACK)
Quibdas (QUEEB-DAZ)
Paras (PAH-RAZ)
Thariel (THAR-EE-ELL)

To Distract Attention

Symiel under Demoriel

In some cases, being less visible is not desirable. If you're working in a place where you need to be seen and noticed, the best alternative is to make others look the other way when you are doing something clandestine. The difference is small, but it means people can remain aware of you, but when they are about to perceive that which you intend to hide, they become distracted by other things and other thoughts. This can make the people around you seem somewhat scatterbrained at times.

Using this ritual, you can openly flirt with somebody at a social gathering, and your spouse and friends will not notice. You can undermine somebody you work with, and everybody will look the other way as you scheme and put things in place.

In theory, the ritual works for as long as you are engaged in the named activity, whether it lasts for an evening or a decade.

You are required, however, to name the situation. With that flirting example, you could say, 'Every time I flirt at a party,' or it may just be that you're planning something special at one particular party. Either approach will work, but use the one you actually mean at the time.

The opening chant is made to the Emperor Demon Demoriel (DEM-OAR-EE-ELL). The request is spoken to the Demon of Adjuration Symiel (SIM-EE-ELL).

Demoriel (DEM-OAR-EE-ELL)

Carnol (CAR-KNOLL)
Menador (MEN-ADORE)
Burisiel (BOO-REE-SEE-ELL)
Arnibiel (ARE-NIB-EE-ELL)
Diriel (DEE-REE-ELL)
Dubilon (DO-BEE-LAWN)
Medar (MED-ARE)

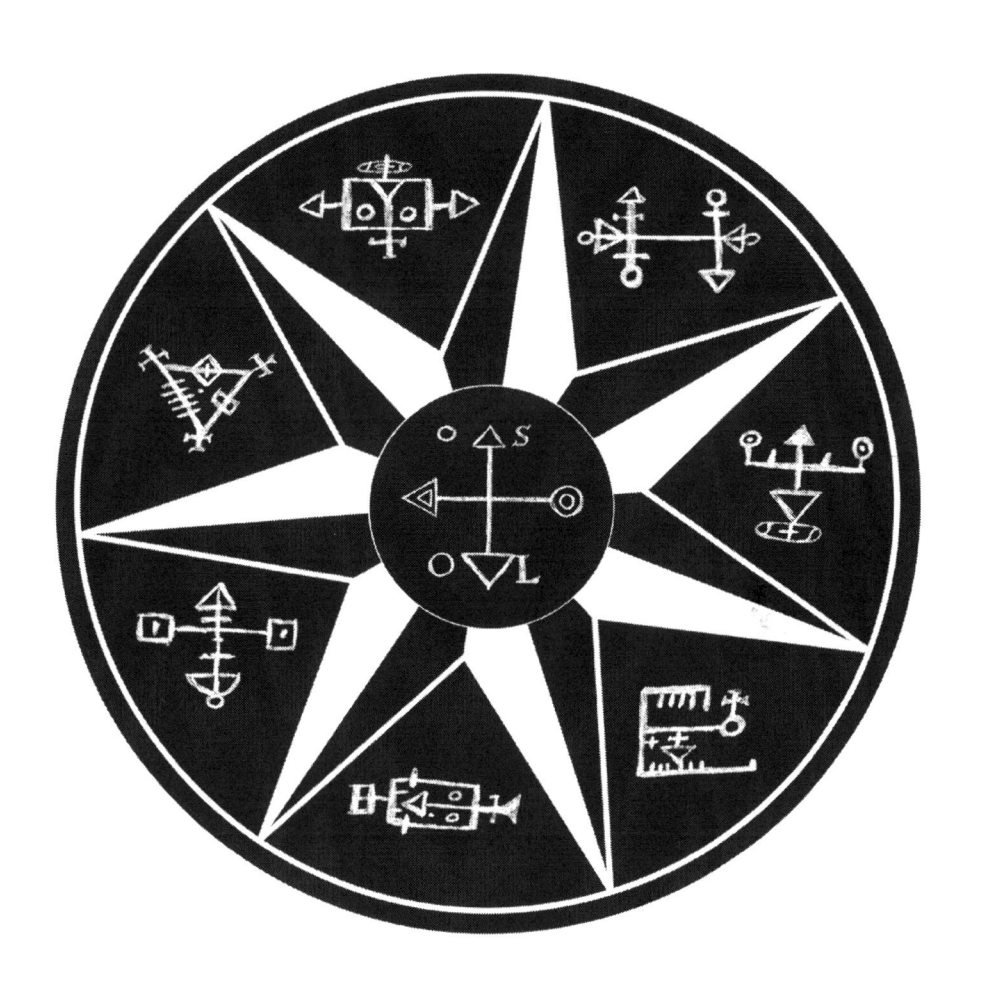

Symiel (SIM-EE-ELL)

Arafos (AH-RA-FORCE)
Narzael (NAR-ZA-ELL)
Murahe (MOO-RAH-HEE)
Curiel (COO-REE-ELL)
Molael (MAW-LAH-ELL)
Nalael (NAH-LAH-ELL)
Richel (RICK-ELL)

To Blur the Truth

Armadiel under Demoriel

This ritual can be used against anybody who has evidence that could harm you.

The concept that empowers this ritual is the idea that even though a person *has* the evidence, they are unable to understand that evidence themselves, or to speak about it clearly. Somebody could witness you do something in broad daylight, but if you use this ritual against them, they would not be able to speak of it in a convincing way. They will not forget or be confused, but they will not be able to express themselves.

Although this ritual is one of the most powerfully effective in the book, you are constrained by two things. You need to know who may speak out about you, and you need to know (roughly) when they may do so. This means that a court appearance is ideal, so long as you know the names of the witness that is being called. You know the date, you know the name, so you tell the demon to blur the truth for that person at that time. If, however, you were accused of something at your place of work, but you have no idea who has evidence against you, this ritual wouldn't work, and you'd need to turn to other types of deception and confusion.

The opening chant is made to the Emperor Demon Demoriel (DEM-OAR-EE-ELL). The request is spoken to the Demon of Adjuration Armadiel (ARM-AH-DEE-ELL).

Demoriel (DEM-OAR-EE-ELL)

Diriel (DEE-REE-ELL)
Menador (MEN-ADORE)
Arnibiel (ARE-NIB-EE-ELL)
Burisiel (BOO-REE-SEE-ELL)
Carnol (CAR-KNOLL)
Dubilon (DO-BEE-LAWN)
Medar (MED-ARE)

Armadiel (ARM-AH-DEE-ELL)

Pandiel (PAN-DEE-ELL)
Massar (MASS-ARE)
Asmael (AZ-MAH-ELL)
Calvarnia (CAL-VARN-EE-AH)
Carasiba (CAH-RAH-SEE-BAH)
Iaziel (EE-AZ-EE-ELL)
Oeniel (AWE-EN-EE-ELL)

To Move Attention to Another

Baruchas under Demoriel

This is a particularly unpleasant operation, because it involves making suspicion pass to somebody else. Once again, let us imagine that you're working in an office environment, and you have done wrong. Despite your efforts, suspicion is being directed at you. To avoid being caught, you use this ritual to turn suspicion onto somebody else.

The ritual can be used as a last resort, when it looks like the game is up, or as a first weapon, to make sure that those who might catch you waste time investigating somebody else. Even if there's no actual investigation, this can make somebody else take the blame, keeping your reputation intact.

The ritual works, but its main limitation is that you have no control over where suspicion will fall. This means that if your best friend works in the same office, your best friend may become the subject of an investigation. Ponder the pitfalls and hidden traps of this ritual before you go ahead. If you don't care who takes the fall, then it works beautifully.

Your task is to instruct the demon to direct attention away from a named situation (summarized as well as you can), to leave you at peace. This means the demon will choose somebody who will not be immediately cleared of suspicion, giving you more time to cover your tracks.

The opening chant is made to the Emperor Demon Demoriel (DEM-OAR-EE-ELL). The request is spoken to the Demon of Adjuration Baruchas (BAH-ROO-KAZ).

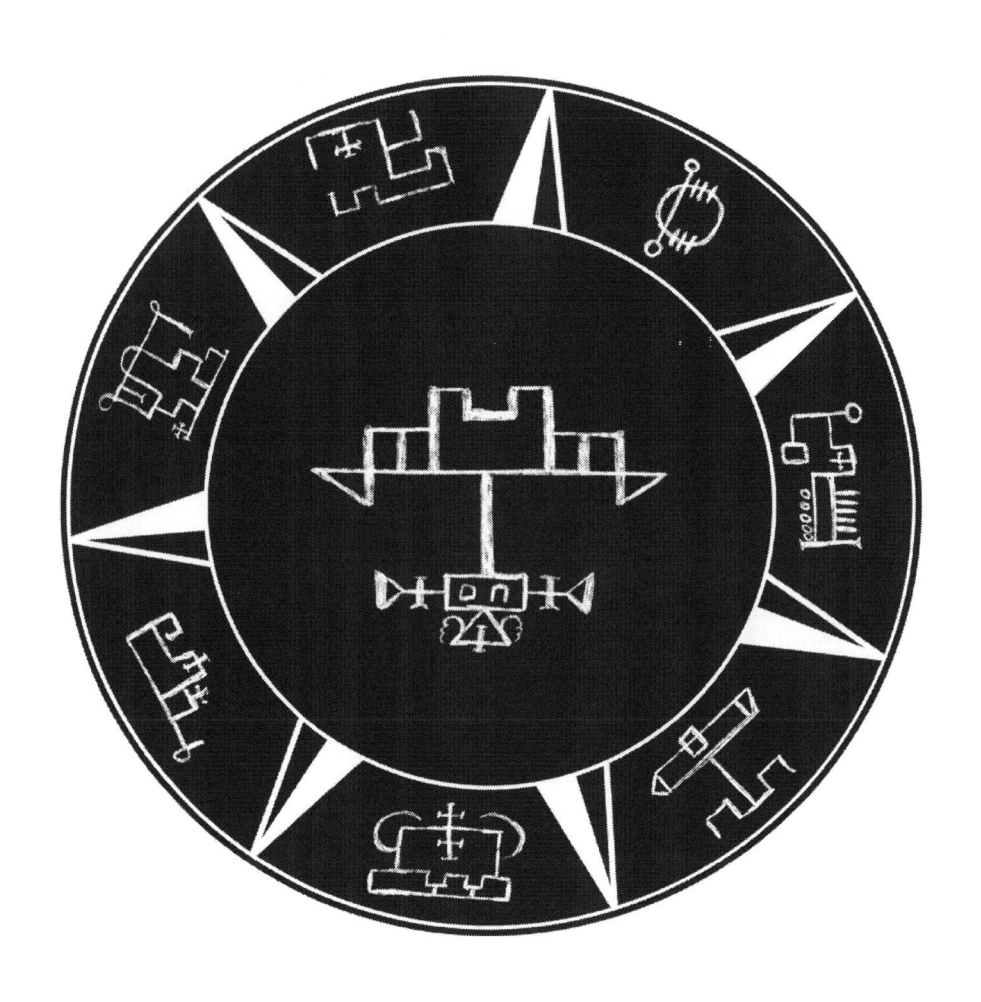

Demoriel (DEM-OAR-EE-ELL)

Medar (MED-ARE)
Burisiel (BOO-REE-SEE-ELL)
Arnibiel (ARE-NIB-EE-ELL)
Menador (MEN-ADORE)
Diriel (DEE-REE-ELL)
Dubilon (DO-BEE-LAWN)
Carnol (CAR-KNOLL)

Baruchas (BAH-ROO-KAZ)

Cartael (CAR-TAH-ELL)
Geriel (GEH-REE-ELL)
Ianiel (EE-AH-NEE-ELL)
Monael (MAW-NAH-ELL)
Decaniel (DECK-AH-NEE-ELL)
Pharol (FAR-ALL)
Aboc (AB-OCK)

Ongoing Magick

There is great potential here, but don't let the nature of the magick tempt you into thoughtless acts. If you attempt to lead a life of petty crime (with magick used to cover your tracks), you're really missing the point, because minor criminal acts are not required by those who have magick on their side. But I imagine that this book will be of interest mostly to those who live complex lives, who need secrecy in times of trouble, when exploring new possibilities, and when personal space is required to achieve a new life or to gain an advantage.

If you buy the book to hide a single act, or to cover up one misdeed, don't let it end there. The potential of this magick is greatest when put into place skillfully, deliberately, as you plan your next move. I don't think I need to say much more about that, now that I have drawn your attention to it. If you want your life to expand, the tools you require to make the right moves, without being seen, are at your disposal.

Although you should put great faith in this magick, do not let down your guard. The magick complements your efforts to maintain secrecy. It is true that I have seen people get away with unbelievable acts, right under the noses of those who are trying to catch them out. But be wise. Don't tempt disaster by assuming the magick lets you become casual with secrecy. The magick works best when you are thoroughly engaged in maintaining a deception, rather than hoping the magick will do everything for you. I point this out because the power can go to your head. When you see that you can deceive, when somebody who should suspect you believes in you, it can be very tempting to toy with the power. If you do, you may get away with it, and good luck to you. But remember that the power to achieve what you actually want is more useful than wallowing in displays of personal power.

If you change your mind after performing a ritual, or wish for the effects to come to an end, for whatever reason, write a new request stating this, and repeat the ritual with your new request. Tell the demon clearly that you wish for the effects of your previous ritual to come to an end. Be very careful, though, as this can uncover your previously hidden secrets. The technique is only explained here because I am sure some people will change their minds, and will want to know how to end the magick's effects.

I hope and believe that you will find this to be a practical book, with more potential than may at first seem obvious. It might be difficult to openly enthuse about the powers of this book, because they are subtle. When it works, nothing happens. That is, you don't get caught. Do a money spell, you get some cash and it's a big, obvious result. Do a deception ritual, and the best you can hope for is that nothing at all happens. Take the time to notice when it's worked well, because demons are vain, and although the demons in this book seek no reward other than the attention you give them during the ritual, they certainly work more readily and powerfully when they sense your appreciation. With this system, you never need to offer up rewards or gifts, or call the demons directly to give thanks, or even remember their names; but a mild, personal feeling of appreciation, when you feel your secret is safe, when you know that the magick has worked – that helps the magick stay secure, and helps future magick work more easily.

At times, you may be confused about which magick to use. There are sixteen rituals on offer, and working out which to use is an important part of your magickal work. The descriptions I have given are brief, to avoid an overwhelm of information, but their brevity means that you are required to put some effort in. Choose carefully. Read about the powers, and think carefully about what you actually need. It may be one ritual. It may be several. Do what needs to be done, with full conviction, and no more. Know that it will work.

The examples I have used are mundane. Office environments. Casual affairs. These may be your concerns, and they are valid. But I will say this once, plainly. The magick can be used in places of great power, and in situations where immense change can take place. The potential of the magick is only hinted at in these petty illustrations, and if you are to thrive, grow and build a life of power, you should think far beyond the examples that I have given.

One final warning. Avoid the temptation to boast. I have known people on both sides of the law tell stories of those who almost completely avoided detection, until their pride led them to boast. Secrecy and deception begin with your own ability to remain silent, and the magick will not keep you silent. Boasting is a dangerous weakness, as it not only reveals too much, but engenders jealousy, leading even trusted friends to spill the beans. When you want to deceive, or keep secrets, be secretive and deceptive.

Years of research and experiment went into perfecting this

work. Even the process of obtaining my own copies of the seals was very drawn out (you can hardly imagine!), and then the lengthy interpretation and experimentation became a huge project that has taken extreme amounts of time, effort, courage and patience. I appreciate the financial sacrifice you have made to access this knowledge, but please know that if you review this book on Amazon, you help support the ongoing creation of this kind of book. Without supportive readers, the secrets remain hidden, so I genuinely appreciate your efforts to let others know that this magick works.

Sincerely,

Corwin Hargrove

Printed in Poland
by Amazon Fulfillment
Poland Sp. z o.o., Wrocław